We Can

by Carolyn Lee
illustrated by Chris Lensch

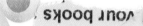

Sell your books

We are baby birds.
We can fly in the sky.

We are baby bats.
We can fly in the sky, too.

We are baby penguins.
We can slide on the ice.

We are baby bears.
We can slide on the
ice, too.

We are baby kangaroos.
We can hop under
the tree.

We are baby bunnies.
We can hop under the
tree, too.

We can move!

It Moves!

Choose one animal from the book.

What can it do? Where can it move?

Tell your partner.

 ## Animal Moves

Draw a picture of a different animal.

Show how it moves.

Write about your picture.

The _____ can move.

Get Up and Go!

GR C • Benchmark 3 • Lexile 140

Grade K • Unit 1 Week 2

www.mheonline.com

The **McGraw·Hill** Companies

ISBN-13 978-0-02-119428-5
MHID 0-02-119428-9

99701

EAN

9 780021 194285

K

STRATEGIES & SKILLS

Comprehension
   Strategy: Ask and Answer Questions
   Skill: Key Details

Phonics
   short *a*

High-Frequency Words
   we

Word count: 66

Education

Copyright © The McGraw-Hill Companies, Inc.

All rights reserved. No part of this publication may be reproduced or distributed in any form or by any means, or stored in a database or retrieval system, without the prior written consent of The McGraw-Hill Companies, Inc., including, but not limited to, network storage or transmission, or broadcast for distance learning.

Send all inquiries to:
McGraw-Hill Education
Two Penn Plaza
New York, New York 10121

ISBN: 978-0-02-119428-5
MHID: 0-02-119428-9

Printed in the United States.

6 7 8 9 DOC 17 16 15 14

B

Fiction

We Can Move!

by Carolyn Lee
illustrated by Chris Lensch

McGraw Hill